KT-370-362

pancakes

pancakes

hamlyn

First published in 2002 by Hamlyn,
a division of Octopus Publishing Group Limited
2–4 Heron Quays, London, E14 4JP

Copyright © 2002 Octopus Publishing Group Limited

All rights reserved. No part of this publication may be
reproduced, stored in a retrieval system or transmitted
in any form or by any means, electronic, mechanical,
photocopying, recording or otherwise, without the
prior written permission of the publisher.

ISBN 0 600 60510 8

Printed and bound in China

10 9 8 7 6 5 4 3 2 1

Photographer: Gus Filgate
Food Stylist: Joanna Farrow

Notes

Standard level spoon measures are used in all
recipes
1 tablespoon = one 15 ml spoon
1 teaspoon = one 5 ml spoon

Both metric and imperial measurements are
given for the recipes. Use one set of
measures only, not a mixture of both.

Ovens should be preheated to the specified
temperature. If using a fan-assisted oven,
follow the manufacturer's instructions for
adjusting the time and temperature. Grills
should also be preheated.

Pepper should be freshly ground unless
otherwise specified.

Free-range medium eggs should be used
unless otherwise specified. The Department
of Health advises that eggs should not be
consumed raw. This book contains dishes
made with raw or lightly cooked eggs. It is
prudent for more vulnerable people such as
pregnant and nursing mothers, invalids, the
elderly, babies and young children to avoid
uncooked or lightly cooked dishes made with
eggs. Once prepared, these dishes should be
kept refrigerated and used promptly.

Use full-fat milk unless otherwise suggested.

Fresh herbs should be used unless otherwise
stated. If unobtainable, use dried herbs as an
alternative but halve the quantities stated.

A few recipes include nuts and nut
derivatives. Anyone with a known nut allergy
must avoid these. Children under the age of
three with a family history of nut allergy,
asthma, eczema or any other type of allergy
are also advised to avoid eating dishes that
contain nuts.

contents

introduction

Inexpensive and easy to make from storecupboard ingredients, pancakes – in one form or another – have been fried, rolled around all kinds of fillings or served plain in dozens of countries throughout the world. But it was, perhaps inevitably, France that raised this modest little dish to greater culinary heights. Although now best known as a dessert, pancakes were traditionally served as an appetizer. They were filled with ham, cheese, mushrooms or seafood, often coated in a creamy sauce. At some time, different parts of France began to produce their own specialities and both Brittany and Agen have laid claim to being the first region to serve them at the end rather than the beginning of a meal.

Throughout the Christian world, pancakes are traditionally cooked on Shrove Tuesday, the day before the Lenten fast begins. It has often been suggested that this close association resulted from frugal housewives using up their stocks of eggs and butter before they were banned for the next forty days and undoubtedly there is an element of truth in this. However, the symbolism of pancakes is much greater than mere practicality and each of the ingredients bears a special significance. Flour is the staff of life, eggs represent creation, milk symbolizes purity and salt is a sign of wholesomeness. Many

French families still carry out the traditional custom of making a wish, while touching the handle of the pan with one hand, holding a coin and turning the pancake with the other. In England, pancake races and other games are relics of a more riotous celebration. European Catholics also serve pancakes on Candlemas Day – 2nd February – as a symbol of renewal and hope.

Of course, pancakes are eaten and enjoyed throughout the year. Crêperies, or pancake houses, have spread from their native Brittany to Germany, Austria, Britain and the United States. One restaurant in the Belgian city of Bruges even claims to serve the biggest selection of pancakes in the world. For the home cook, pancakes are the perfect solution to the perennial question of what to serve for the family's supper. Always popular, they can provide a quick, substantial and inexpensive main course, filled with bacon, chicken, prawns, spinach, courgettes, tomatoes, cheese or mushrooms, or a delicious treat for dessert, sprinkled with sugar and lemon juice, smothered in syrup, filled with fruit or flavoured with chocolate. They may even be cut into thin strips and used to garnish soup, or stacked, layered with cream, jam or fruit, to make a cake.

Choosing a pan

As with any task, using the right equipment to cook pancakes is of the utmost importance. It is possible to cook pancakes in a standard frying pan, but they risk being uneven, they may stick, and are more difficult to turn and so more likely to break up. Using a special pancake or crêpe pan, which is smaller and has a smooth base and gently sloping curved sides, virtually guarantees success. The most popular size is 18–20 cm (7–8 inches), but you can also buy pans as large as 25 cm (10 inches). Note that these measurements refer to the diameter of the rim of the pan and not to the size of the pancake. Pans may be made of a variety of materials, but it is important that they are heavy so the batter cooks quickly and evenly. It is worth buying the best pan you can afford, as cheap pans are a false economy because they will soon buckle and become useless. Keep your pan exclusively for cooking pancakes; if you use it to fry other foods, you may spoil the essential smoothness of the base. Always follow the manufacturer's instructions for cleaning the pan after use; these will vary depending on the metal used and on whether it has a nonstick lining.

Traditional pans were made of cast iron and some cooks maintain that these pans are still the best for pancakes

made with buckwheat flour. They take quite a long time to heat up, but distribute the heat very evenly. You will need to season a new cast-iron pan. Sprinkle a layer of salt over the base and heat gently. Tip out the excess salt and rub the pan with a little vegetable oil, using kitchen paper. Be careful not to burn your hand. Leave the pan slightly oily before using it for the first time. If the pan is well seasoned, you will need very little oil for cooking pancakes. If possible, do not wash the pan after use; simply wipe it clean with kitchen paper. If later you need to season it again, wash it thoroughly in hot water and detergent, dry it well and repeat the process.

Heavy gauge steel pans are also available, although they are more often labelled omelette pans rather than pancake or crêpe pans. Nevertheless, they are still the same shape with a flat base and sloping sides. Steel pans are expensive and should be treated with respect. They need careful seasoning with vegetable oil alone. Like cast-iron pans, they should not be washed, but simply wiped clean with kitchen paper and then oiled again before storage to prevent rusting.

While seasoning a cast-iron or steel pan effectively makes it nonstick, many people prefer to play safe and use a more modern pan with a synthetic resin coating, such as Teflon, or a hard-anodized lining. These pans are usually made of heavy-gauge aluminium and the nonstick lining is very smooth and durable. Use wooden spatulas and tools to avoid scratching the surface and never clean these pans with anything abrasive that may damage the coating.

When buying a pan, it is always worth checking the firmness of the handle. If it is not securely welded or riveted, you not only risk ruining your pancakes, but also burning yourself. Some pans are cast in one piece with their handles and, while these are very secure, the handles are likely to become quite hot.

Tabletop, electric, nonstick crêpe pans are also available, but these are more suitable for use in restaurants than at home – unless you are addicted to Crêpes Suzette and other flambéed pancakes. Most have a flat pan in which the batter is cooked in the conventional way, but some have a convex base, which is first dipped in the batter and then reversed for cooking.

Ingredients

Basic pancake batter consists of plain flour, salt, eggs and milk. Buckwheat flour may be substituted for half the plain flour. Some cooks prefer to use a mixture of equal parts of milk and water, rather than milk alone – water makes the pancakes very light, milk makes the batter smooth and helps the pancakes turn golden brown. Using half beer and half milk will make the pancakes rise slightly and gives them a savoury flavour. Light chicken stock may also be included in the liquid. For a richer batter, you can add an extra egg to the basic recipe, but reduce the quantity of milk by 2 tablespoons.

Batter for dessert pancakes can also include a little caster or vanilla sugar. Individual recipes may specify additional ingredients. Plain chocolate can be melted in the milk, for example, or a spoonful of brandy or liqueur can be whisked into it for extra flavour. Finely grated citrus rind, orange or lemon juice, orange flower water, ground cinnamon, mixed spice and almond or vanilla essence are also popular additions.

Stirring 1–2 tablespoons of melted butter or bland-tasting vegetable oil, such as groundnut or safflower, into the batter just before cooking the pancakes gives them a rich flavour and also helps to prevent them from sticking to the pan. Always use unsalted butter for dessert pancakes.

Batters may also be made with yeast, although these are more often used for coatings than for pancakes. Russian blinis are probably the best-known example of yeast pancakes, but these are unlike the more familiar rolled or folded filled pancakes. Light and airy, they are small and usually served with a topping, frequently smoked salmon or caviar and soured cream.

Pancakes may be fried in oil or melted butter. Again, it is best to use a bland vegetable oil or unsalted butter. If the pan has a nonstick finish or has been well seasoned, it will require no more than the occasional light brushing with oil or butter, depending on how many pancakes you are cooking.

How to make the perfect pancake

Basic pancake batter can be used for both savoury and sweet dishes and the technique remains the same when making flavoured batters. The secret of success is to avoid over-beating the batter. Beat the ingredients only until they are combined and smooth. Too much whisking causes the gluten in the flour to develop and, as a result, the pancakes will be tough and chewy. The exception is when making yeast batter, which requires vigorous beating to develop the gluten. When following any pancake recipe, you may need to adjust the quantity of liquid you add to the batter, as individual flours will vary. Aim to achieve a fairly thin, pouring consistency.

It is not essential to let the batter rest before cooking the pancakes, but it does produce a lighter result. Pancakes made from freshly prepared batter tend to have a bubbly, rather than a flat surface. Pour the batter into a jug, cover and set aside in a cool place for about 30 minutes to allow the starch in the flour to swell. If the batter has begun to separate when you are ready to cook the pancakes, stir it well to remix but do not overmix. If the batter has been standing for a longer period, it may have thickened and you will need to stir in a little more liquid. Do not leave the batter

to stand for more than 12 hours or it will begin to ferment.

As each pancake is cooked, slide it out of the pan on to a warm flat plate. Stack the pancakes, interleaved with greaseproof paper or nonstick baking paper, and keep them warm over a pan of gently simmering water or in a very low oven.

Storing pancakes

If the pancakes are to be used straight away, simply stack them on a plate and keep them warm. If you are making them ahead to use later in the day or to store overnight in the refrigerator, interleave them with nonstick baking paper to prevent them sticking together. To freeze pancakes, interleave with nonstick baking paper and wrap in foil. They can be frozen for up to 3 months. They will also keep in the refrigerator, wrapped in the same way, for up to 2 days. To serve, thaw frozen pancakes overnight in the refrigerator, then reheat in a pan over a low heat or in a low oven.

Filling and serving pancakes

Unlike omelettes, most pancakes are not filled while still in the pan. There are a few exceptions, such as egg and cheese pancakes, when an egg is cracked on top of a just cooked pancake and then sprinkled with cheese once it has set, before the pancake is folded and tipped out of the pan. More usually, the filling is simply spooned into the pancake, which is then rolled or folded into a neat parcel. After folding, savoury

pancakes may be covered with a sauce, sprinkled with grated cheese and briefly baked in the oven. These are ways to fold sweet or savoury pancakes:

The basic roll Lay the pancake on a plate or work surface and spoon some filling in a ribbon down the centre. Fold one side of the pancake over the filling to cover it, then the other side over the first to form a neat roll with the filling showing at both ends.

The cigarette Lay the pancake flat and spread the filling thinly over the whole of it. Starting at one edge, roll the pancake into a long, thin cylinder.

The parcel Lay the pancake flat and place a spoonful of filling in the centre of it. Fold both sides over the filling, then fold the bottom edge over it. Finally, fold the top edge down to make a neat parcel. Turn over and serve.

The baton Lay the pancake flat and spoon some filling into the centre of it. Fold over both sides to cover the filling, then roll up the pancake from the bottom to form a neat roll.

The triangle Fold the pancake in half and in half again to form a triangle. Stuff one of the pockets with filling and serve.

The stack Lay a pancake on a serving plate and spread with some filling. Lay another pancake on top, then top with more filling. Continue until all the filling and all the pancakes have been used.

basic pancakes

125 g (4 oz) plain flour

pinch of salt

1 egg, lightly beaten

300 ml (½ pint) milk

light olive oil, vegetable oil or
butter, for greasing the pan

These plain pancakes can be used for any savoury pancake recipe, or dessert recipes where you don't want too sweet or rich a flavour.

1 Put the flour and salt into a bowl and make a well in the centre. Pour the egg and a little of the milk into the well. Whisk the liquid, gradually incorporating the flour to make a smooth paste. Whisk in the remaining milk then pour the batter into a jug. Allow to rest, if liked.

2 Put a little oil or butter into an 18 cm (7 inch) pancake pan or heavy-based frying pan and heat until it starts to smoke. Pour off the excess oil and pour a little batter into the pan, tilting the pan until the base is coated in a thin layer. (If you prefer, use a small ladle to measure the batter into the pan.) Cook for 1–2 minutes until the underside is turning golden.

3 Flip the pancake with a palette knife and cook for a further 30–45 seconds until it is golden on the second side. Slide the pancake out of the pan and make the remaining pancakes, oiling the pan as necessary.

Makes 8–10 pancakes
Preparation time: **5 minutes, plus resting (optional)**
Cooking time: **15–25 minutes**

variations

Spinach pancakes
Trim the stalks from 250 g (8 oz) washed spinach leaves and put the leaves, with just the water clinging to them, into a heavy-based saucepan. Cover the pan with a lid and cook the spinach over a gentle heat for 2 minutes or until wilted. Drain thoroughly, pressing out any excess water. Chop finely and beat into the batter with the milk.

Herb pancakes
Finely chop a small handful of fresh herbs such as parsley, basil, tarragon, dill, chervil or oregano. Beat into the batter.

Wholemeal pancakes
Replace the plain flour with wholemeal flour, or, for a lighter alternative, use half wholemeal and half plain flour.

buckwheat pancakes

125 g (4 oz) buckwheat flour

pinch of salt

3 eggs, lightly beaten

300 ml (½ pint) milk

light olive oil, vegetable oil or
butter, for greasing the pan

These have a richer, nuttier flavour than pancakes made with white flour and are delicious in both sweet and savoury recipes. Buckwheat flour is widely available in supermarkets and health food stores.

1 Put the flour and salt into a bowl and make a well in the centre. Add the eggs and a little of the milk and whisk together, gradually incorporating the flour. Add the remaining milk and mix to a smooth paste. Pour into a jug. Allow to rest, if liked.

2 Put a little oil or butter into an 18 cm (7 inch) pancake pan or heavy-based frying pan and heat until it starts to smoke. Pour off the excess and pour a little batter into the pan, tilting the pan until the base is coated in a thin layer. (If you prefer, use a small ladle to measure the batter into the pan.) Cook for 1–2 minutes until the underside is turning golden.

3 Flip the pancake with a palette knife and cook for a further 30–45 seconds until golden on the second side. Slide the pancake out of the pan and make the remaining pancakes, greasing the pan as necessary.

Makes 8–10 pancakes
Preparation time: **5 minutes, plus resting (optional)**
Cooking time: **15–25 minutes**

sweet pancakes

125 g (4 oz) plain flour

pinch of salt

2 tablespoons caster sugar

1 egg, lightly beaten

300 ml (½ pint) milk

25 g (1 oz) unsalted butter, melted

light olive oil, vegetable oil or butter, for greasing the pan

1 Put the flour, salt and sugar into a bowl and make a well in the centre. Pour the egg and a little of the milk into the well. Whisk the liquid, gradually incorporating the flour to make a smooth paste. Whisk in the butter, then the remaining milk until smooth. Pour the batter into a jug. Allow to rest, if liked.

2 Put a little oil or butter in an 18 cm (7 inch) pancake pan or heavy-based frying pan and heat until it starts to smoke. Pour off the excess and pour a little batter into the pan, tilting the pan until the base is coated in a thin layer. (If you prefer, use a small ladle to measure the batter into the pan.) Cook for 1–2 minutes until the underside is turning golden.

3 Flip the pancake with a palette knife and cook for a further 30–45 seconds until golden on the second side. Slide the pancake out of the pan and make the remaining pancakes, greasing the pan as necessary.

Makes 8–10 pancakes
Preparation time: **5 minutes, plus resting (optional)**
Cooking time: **15–25 minutes**

lemon and cinnamon pancakes

15 g (½ oz) butter

125 g (4 oz) plain flour

½ teaspoon ground cinnamon

pinch of salt

1 teaspoon grated lemon rind

1 egg, beaten

300 ml (½ pint) milk

vegetable oil or butter, for frying

to serve:

sugar

lemon wedges

1 Melt the butter in a small pan. Sift the flour, cinnamon, salt and grated lemon rind into a bowl, make a well in the centre and gradually beat in the egg, milk and melted butter to make a smooth batter.

2 Put a little oil or butter in an 18 cm (7 inch) pancake pan or heavy-based frying pan and heat until it starts to smoke. Pour off the excess and pour a little batter into the pan, tilting it until the base is coated in a thin layer. (Or, if you prefer, use a small ladle to measure the batter into the pan.) Cook for 1–2 minutes until the underside begins to turn golden.

3 Flip the pancake with a palette knife and cook for a further 30–45 seconds until golden on the second side. Slide the pancake out of the pan and make the remaining pancakes, greasing the pan as necessary.

4 Serve 2–3 pancakes per person, dusted with sugar and accompanied with lemon wedges.

Makes 8 pancakes
Preparation time: **5 minutes**
Cooking time: **15–25 minutes**

wholemeal honey pancakes

125 g (4 oz) wholemeal self-raising flour

1 egg, beaten

300 ml (½ pint) milk

4 tablespoons clear honey

50 g (2 oz) seedless raisins

pinch of grated nutmeg

1 Put the flour into a bowl and make a well in the centre. Pour in the egg and milk and beat to a smooth batter. In another bowl, mix together the honey, raisins and nutmeg.

2 Using a lightly greased pancake pan and the batter, cook 8 pancakes (*see page* 12) and keep them warm. Spread each pancake with a spoonful of the mixture, and then fold to form a wedge-shaped parcel. Serve immediately.

Makes 8 pancakes
Preparation time: **5–10 minutes**
Cooking time: **15–25 minutes**

chocolate pancakes

100 g (3½ oz) plain flour

15 g (½ oz) cocoa powder

2 tablespoons caster sugar

1 egg

300 ml (½ pint) milk

vegetable oil or butter, for frying

1 Sift the flour and cocoa powder into a bowl then stir in the sugar. Add the egg and a little milk, and whisk to make a stiff batter. Beat in the remaining milk.

2 Put a little oil or butter in a 18 cm (7 inch) pancake pan or heavy-based frying pan and heat until it starts to smoke. Pour off the excess and pour a little batter into the pan, tilting it until the base is coated in a thin layer. (Or, if you prefer, use a small ladle to measure the batter into the pan.) Cook for 1–2 minutes until the underside begins to turn golden.

3 Flip the pancake with a palette knife and cook for a further 30–45 seconds on the second side. Slide the pancake out of the pan and make the remaining pancakes, greasing the pan as necessary.

Makes about 8 pancakes
Preparation time: **5–10 minutes**
Cooking time: **15–25 minutes**

courgette pancakes with emmental cheese and pepper sauce

1 quantity Basic Pancake batter (*see page* 12)

1 tablespoon chopped thyme

325 g (11 oz) courgettes, grated

6 tablespoons olive oil

300 g (10 oz) aubergine, cut into small chunks

2 small red onions, sliced

2 red peppers, cored, deseeded and sliced

400 g (13 oz) can chopped tomatoes

2 tablespoons balsamic vinegar

300 g (10 oz) Emmental or Gruyère cheese, thinly sliced

oil or butter, for frying

salt and pepper

These crisp little pancakes, topped with melting cheese and a ratatouille-style mixture, make a very good starter. Alternatively, you can make larger pancakes and serve them with a salad for a delicious main course.

1 Pour the pancake batter into a large bowl and stir in the thyme and the grated courgettes. Season with salt and pepper. Set aside.

2 Heat the olive oil in a large heavy-based saucepan or frying pan. Add the aubergine and onions and fry for about 5 minutes until turning golden. Add the peppers and continue frying quickly for about 3 minutes until the vegetables are lightly browned. Add the tomatoes and vinegar and season with salt and pepper. Reduce the heat and simmer gently, uncovered, for 10 minutes while cooking the pancakes.

3 Heat a little oil or butter in a large frying pan. Add 1 tablespoon of the pancake mixture to one side of the pan and spread to around 10 cm (4 inches) across. Add as many more spoonfuls of batter as the pan will hold and fry for about 2 minutes or until golden on the underside. Flip the pancakes and cook for 2 minutes longer. Drain on kitchen paper and transfer to a grill pan. Cook the remainder of the pancakes (the mixture should make 12 in all).

4 Arrange the cheese slices over the pancakes and cook under a preheated hot grill until the cheese has melted. Arrange 2 pancakes on each serving plate, overlapping them slightly. Pile the pepper sauce on top and serve warm.

Serves 6
Preparation time: **10 minutes, plus making the pancake batter**
Cooking time: **20–25 minutes**

spinach and ricotta pancakes

1 quantity Basic Pancakes
(*see page* 12)

250 g (8 oz) cooked spinach

1 egg, beaten

250 g (8 oz) ricotta cheese

50 g (2 oz) Parmesan cheese,
grated

25 g (1 oz) butter

5 tablespoons chicken or
vegetable stock

salt and pepper

1 Make the pancakes and set them aside while making the filling.

2 Chop the spinach. Stir in the egg, ricotta and half the Parmesan. Season with salt and pepper. Divide the mixture among the pancakes, roll them up and put them into a lightly greased shallow ovenproof dish. Dot with the butter and the remaining cheese and add the stock. Bake in a preheated oven, 200°C (400°F), Gas Mark 6, for 20 minutes. Serve immediately.

Makes about 8 pancakes
Preparation time: **10 minutes, plus making the pancakes**
Cooking time: **20 minutes**

spinach pancakes with asparagus

24 thick asparagus spears, trimmed

8 Spinach Pancakes (*see page* 13)

vegetable oil, for greasing

50 g (2 oz) Cheshire cheese, grated

béchamel sauce:

300 ml (½ pint) milk

1 small onion, roughly chopped

1 bay leaf

25 g (1 oz) butter

25 g (1 oz) plain flour

salt and pepper

1 First make the béchamel sauce. Put the milk, onion and bay leaf into a saucepan and heat until just boiling. Remove from the heat and set aside for 20 minutes to infuse. Strain the milk and reserve. Meanwhile, make the pancakes and keep them warm.

2 Melt the butter in a saucepan, stir in the flour and cook over a low heat for 1 minute. Remove from the heat and beat in the infused milk, a little at a time, until blended. Return to a low heat and stir constantly until thickened. Bring to a gentle boil, stirring, then simmer for 2 minutes. Season with salt and pepper.

3 Blanch the asparagus spears in a large pan of lightly salted boiling water for 2 minutes. Drain and pat dry on kitchen paper.

4 Place 3 asparagus spears on each pancake and roll them up. Place the pancakes seam-side down in a lightly greased, shallow ovenproof dish. Pour over the béchamel sauce and sprinkle with the cheese.

5 Place the dish under a preheated moderately hot grill and cook for 8–10 minutes until bubbling and golden. Serve at once.

Serves 4
Preparation time: **10 minutes, plus making the pancakes and infusing the milk**
Cooking time: **15–20 minutes**

savoury florentine layer

8 Herb Pancakes (*see page* 13)

tomato filling:

250 g (8 oz) canned tomatoes

15 g (½ oz) butter

1 onion, chopped

2 garlic cloves, finely chopped

75 g (3 oz) Parmesan cheese, grated, plus extra for sprinkling

2 tablespoons chopped oregano

salt and pepper

spinach filling:

500 g (1 lb) baby spinach

25 g (1 oz) butter

2 tablespoons milk

1 tablespoon cornflour

150 ml (5 fl oz) single cream

pinch of grated nutmeg

1 Make the pancakes and keep them warm while making the fillings.

2 To make the tomato filling, purée the tomatoes in a food processor or blender or press them through a sieve. Melt the butter in a saucepan, add the onion and cook gently until soft. Add the garlic and cook for 1 minute. Gradually blend in the puréed tomatoes and cook, stirring occasionally, until the mixture thickens. Add the cheese, oregano and salt and pepper to taste then heat gently for 1 minute.

3 To make the spinach filling, wash the spinach and put it into a saucepan with just the water that clings to the leaves. Add the butter, cover the pan and cook gently until wilted. Blend the milk with the cornflour and set aside. Add the cream to the spinach with the nutmeg and salt and pepper to taste. Bring to the boil and simmer for 2 minutes. Stir in the blended cornflour and cook, stirring, until the mixture thickens.

4 To serve, layer the pancakes on a warmed serving platter with alternate layers of the tomato and spinach fillings. Serve hot, sprinkled with a little extra Parmesan and cut into wedges.

Serves 4
Preparation time: **15 minutes, plus making the pancakes**
Cooking time: **20 minutes**

caramelized onion and emmental cheese pancakes

3 tablespoons wholegrain mustard

1 quantity Wholemeal Pancake batter (*see page* 13)

oil or butter, for frying and greasing

filling:

40 g (1½ oz) butter

3 onions, thinly sliced

2 teaspoons caster sugar

a few thyme sprigs

200 g (7 oz) Emmental or Gruyère cheese, grated

salt and pepper

1 Stir the mustard into the pancake batter and cook the pancakes following the instructions on page 12. Set the pancakes aside while making the filling.

2 To make the filling, melt the butter in a heavy-based pan and fry the onions with the sugar for about 8–10 minutes until they are deep golden and caramelized. Tear the thyme leaves from the stems and add them to the pan with salt and plenty of black pepper.

3 Reserve 25 g (1 oz) of the cheese and sprinkle the remainder over the pancakes. Scatter the fried onions over the cheese, then roll up the pancakes and arrange in a lightly greased, shallow ovenproof dish. Sprinkle with the reserved cheese and bake in a preheated oven, 190°C (375°F), Gas Mark 5, for about 15 minutes until the cheese has melted. Serve warm.

Serves 4
Preparation time: **10 minutes, plus making the pancake batter**
Cooking time: **about 40 minutes**

pancakes with wild mushrooms, sherry and cream

25 g (1 oz) dried porcini mushrooms

150 ml (¼ pint) boiling water

1 quantity Basic Pancakes
(*see page* 12)

25 g (1 oz) butter

1 onion, chopped

2 garlic cloves, sliced

250 g (8 oz) chestnut or cup
mushrooms, sliced

1 tablespoon chopped thyme

4 tablespoons chopped flat leaf
parsley

3 tablespoons medium sherry

150 ml (¼ pint) double cream

salt and pepper

spinach or other green vegetables,
to serve

The classic combinaton of mushrooms, sherry and cream makes a lovely filling for pancakes, and is quick and easy to prepare.

1 Put the dried mushrooms into a small bowl, cover with the boiling water and leave to soak for 15 minutes. Meanwhile, make the pancakes and set them aside while making the filling.

2 Melt the butter in a frying pan and fry the onion for 3 minutes. Add the garlic and chestnut mushrooms and fry for 3 minutes. Add the dried mushrooms to the pan with any soaking juices and the herbs, sherry and cream. Season with a little salt and pepper and cook gently for 2 minutes.

3 Fold the pancakes into quarters. Open them out like cones and fill with some of the mushroom mixture. Arrange in a lightly greased, shallow ovenproof dish and bake in a preheated oven, 200°C (400°F), Gas Mark 6, for 15 minutes. Serve on a bed of lightly wilted spinach or other green vegetables.

Serves 4
Preparation time: **20 minutes, plus making the pancakes and soaking the mushrooms**
Cooking time: **30 minutes**

buckwheat pancakes with smoked salmon

4 tablespoons snipped chives

300 ml (½ pint) thick soured cream or crème fraiche

oil or butter, for frying

1 quantity Buckwheat Pancake batter (*see page* 14)

375 g (12 oz) smoked salmon

salt and pepper

to garnish:

chives

lime wedges

1 Mix together the snipped chives, soured cream or crème fraiche and a little salt and pepper and set aside.

2 Heat a little oil or butter in a 15 cm (6 inch) pancake pan or heavy-based frying pan until it starts to smoke. Pour in a little batter, tilting the pan until the base is coated in a thin layer. If you don't have a very small pan use a larger one and let the batter spread to a diameter of about 15 cm (6 inches). Cook for 1–2 minutes until the underside is golden.

3 Flip the pancake with a palette knife and cook for a further 30–45 seconds until golden on the second side. Slide the pancake out of the pan and keep it warm while making the rest, greasing the pan as necessary.

4 To serve, arrange a little smoked salmon on each pancake. Place a spoonful of the cream mixture on the salmon and fold over the pancake to sandwich the filling. Allow 2 or 3 of the pancakes for each person and garnish with chives and lime wedges.

Serves 4
Preparation time: **10 minutes, plus making the pancake batter**
Cooking time: **15–25 minutes**

prawn pancakes with dill and soured cream

8 Basic Pancakes (*see page* 12)

50 g (2 oz) butter

2 fennel heads, thinly sliced

25 g (1 oz) plain flour

300 ml (½ pint) milk

5 tablespoons soured cream

375 g (12 oz) cooked peeled prawns, drained thoroughly

3 tablespoons roughly chopped dill

oil, for greasing

50 g (2 oz) Parmesan cheese, grated

salt and pepper

1 Make the pancakes and keep them warm while making the filling.

2 Melt the butter in a saucepan and fry the fennel slices gently for 5 minutes or until soft. Transfer the fennel to a bowl with a slotted spoon. Add the flour to the pan and cook, stirring, for 1 minute. Gradually whisk in the milk and bring to the boil, whisking until thickened. Remove the pan from the heat, stir in the cream and season with salt and pepper to taste.

3 Add the prawns, dill and 6 tablespoons of the sauce to the fennel and mix together. Spoon the filling over the pancakes and roll them up.

4 Put the pancakes in a lightly greased, shallow ovenproof dish and spoon the remaining sauce down the centre of the pancakes. Sprinkle with the cheese and bake in a preheated oven, 190°C (375°F), Gas Mark 5, for 25 minutes or until the sauce is golden and bubbling.

Serves 4
Preparation time: **10 minutes, plus making the pancakes**
Cooking time: **40 minutes**

oriental-style crab pancake rolls

1 quantity Basic Pancakes
(*see page* 12)

1 tablespoon oil, plus extra
for frying

1 bunch of spring onions, sliced

200 g (7 oz) white cabbage, finely
shredded

2.5 cm (1 inch) piece fresh root
ginger, finely grated

300 g (10 oz) crabmeat

1 teaspoon cornflour

4 tablespoons dry sherry

1 tablespoon Thai fish sauce

1 egg, beaten

salt and pepper

ready-made sweet chilli dipping
sauce, to serve (optional)

These little oriental pancakes make an unusual starter. They should be no more than 15 cm (6 inches) in diameter. Ideally, you should use a small pancake or frying pan, but you could use a larger pan and limit the size of the pancakes.

1 Make the pancakes and keep them warm while making the filling.

2 Heat the oil in a frying pan and fry the spring onions and cabbage for 3 minutes. Transfer the mixture to a bowl and stir in the ginger and crabmeat. Mix the cornflour with the sherry and fish sauce and add to the bowl with a little salt and pepper.

3 Generously brush the edges of a pancake with beaten egg then pile a dessertspoonful of the filling in the centre. Fold the sides over the filling and then roll up the pancake. Repeat with the remaining pancakes and filling.

4 Heat 5 cm (2 inches) of oil in large pan until a piece of bread sizzles on the surface when dropped in. Fry the pancakes, a few at a time, for about 1 minute until golden brown. Drain on kitchen paper and serve with chilli dipping sauce, if liked.

Serves 4
Preparation time: **20 minutes, plus
making the pancakes**
Cooking time: **20 minutes**

turkey, tarragon and mustard pancakes

8 Basic Pancakes (*see page* 12)

50 g (2 oz) butter

1 onion, chopped

2 garlic cloves, crushed

375 g (12 oz) turkey, diced

1 tablespoon Dijon mustard

3 tablespoons roughly chopped tarragon

75 g (3 oz) baby broad beans or peas

150 g (5 oz) crème fraîche

oil, for greasing

50 g (2 oz) mature Cheddar cheese, finely grated

salt and pepper

1 Make the pancakes and keep them warm while making the filling.

2 Melt half of the butter in a frying pan. Add the onion and fry gently for 3 minutes. Add the garlic and turkey and fry for 10 minutes until the turkey is cooked through. Remove the pan from the heat and stir in the mustard, tarragon, broad beans or peas and crème fraîche and season with salt and pepper to taste.

3 Spoon some of the filling down the centre of each pancake and roll them up. Place them in a lightly greased, shallow ovenproof dish. Melt the remaining butter and spoon it over the pancakes. Sprinkle them with the cheese and cover the dish with foil.

4 Bake in a preheated oven, 200°C (400°F), Gas Mark 6, for 15–20 minutes until the pancakes are hot.

Serves 4
Preparation time: **10 minutes, plus making the pancakes**
Cooking time: **35 minutes**

bacon, avocado and soured cream pancakes

8 Basic Pancakes (*see page* 12)

250 g (8 oz) thin streaky bacon rashers

2 avocados

300 ml (½ pint) soured cream

1 garlic clove, crushed

3 tablespoons snipped chives

½ teaspoon mild chilli seasoning

oil, for greasing

125 g (4 oz) Cheddar cheese, finely grated

salt and pepper

1 Make the pancakes and keep them warm while making the filling.

2 Dry-fry the bacon in a heavy-based pan until crisp. Leave it to cool slightly then cut it into small pieces. Halve, stone and peel the avocados and slice them thinly. Mix with the bacon. Beat the soured cream with the garlic, chives, chilli powder and salt and pepper. Stir into the bacon and avocado mixture.

3 Divide the mixture among the pancakes, spreading it thinly to within 1 cm (½ inch) of the edge. Roll up the pancakes and place them in a lightly greased, shallow ovenproof dish.

4 Sprinkle the pancakes with the cheese and bake in a preheated oven, 190°C (375°F), Gas Mark 5, for about 20 minutes until the cheese has melted.

Serves 4
Preparation time: **15 minutes, plus making the pancakes**
Cooking time: **30 minutes**

ham and gruyère pancakes

1 quantity Basic Pancakes
(*see page* 12)

1 quantity Béchamel sauce
(*see page* 20)

50 g (2 oz) Gruyère cheese, grated

300 g (10 oz) sliced ham

oil, for greasing

salt and pepper

1 Make the pancakes and allow to cool while making the filling.

2 Make the sauce, remove the pan from the heat and beat in the grated cheese. Season with salt and pepper and leave the sauce to cool.

3 Divide the ham and the cheese sauce among the pancakes, then roll them up and arrange them in a lightly greased, shallow ovenproof dish. Bake in a preheated oven, 200°C (400°F), Gas Mark 6, for 15 minutes. Serve hot.

Serves 4
Preparation time: **10 minutes, plus making the pancakes and the Béchamel sauce**
Cooking time: **20 minutes**

alsace sausage pancakes

1 quantity Basic Pancake batter
(*see page* 12)

300 g (10 oz) smoked pork sausage, thinly sliced

175 g (6 oz) Gruyère cheese, grated

to garnish:

2 tablespoons chopped parsley

1 shallot, finely chopped

1 garlic clove, crushed

1 Lightly grease a 20 cm (8 inch) pancake pan and heat until very hot. Pour in enough batter to make a very thin pancake, tilting the pan to ensure an even thickness. When the edges begin to brown, cover the pancake with some of the sausage slices and sprinkle with a little cheese.

2 Place under a preheated very hot grill for 20–30 seconds until the cheese melts. Slide the unfolded pancake on to a warmed heatproof platter and keep it hot in a preheated oven, 160°C (325°F), Gas Mark 3, while preparing the remaining pancakes.

3 To serve, mix together the parsley, shallot and garlic and sprinkle over the pancakes.

Serves 6
Preparation time: **5–10 minutes, plus making the pancake batter**
Cooking time: **15–25 minutes**

sweet jam pancakes
with crème anglaise

8 Sweet Pancakes (*see page* 15)

250 g (8 oz) strawberry or raspberry jam

2 tablespoons lemon juice

oil, for greasing

caster sugar, for sprinkling

crème anglaise:

3 egg yolks

2 tablespoons caster sugar

1 teaspoon cornflour

1 teaspoon vanilla essence

300 ml (½ pint) milk

This is a simple and delicious dessert recipe. Crème anglaise is also known as custard cream and vanilla custard; it's a versatile accompaniment which can also be served with fruit salads, soufflés and pies.

1 Make the pancakes and set them aside while making the filling.

2 Melt the jam in a small saucepan with the lemon juice. Spread a little of the mixture over each pancake. Fold them in half, then in half again, and arrange, overlapping, in a lightly greased, shallow ovenproof dish. Bake in a preheated oven, 180°C (350°F), Gas Mark 4, for about 15 minutes until heated through.

3 Meanwhile, make the crème anglaise. Beat the egg yolks in a bowl with the sugar, cornflour, vanilla essence and a little of the milk.

4 Bring the remaining milk to the boil in a heavy-based saucepan. Pour the hot milk over the egg yolk mixture, stirring, then pour it back into the pan. Cook over a very gentle heat, stirring until the crème anglaise has thickened. (Do not boil or the mixture might curdle.) Sprinkle the pancakes with caster sugar and serve with the crème anglaise.

Serves 4
Preparation time: **10 minutes, plus making the pancakes**
Cooking time: **20 minutes**

apple and sultana pancakes

8 Sweet Pancakes (*see page* 15)

5 Granny Smith apples or similar tart dessert apples

40 g (1½ oz) unsalted butter

2 tablespoons flaked almonds

65 g (2½ oz) light muscovado sugar

2 tablespoons lemon juice

50 g (2 oz) sultanas

1 teaspoon ground mixed spice

3 tablespoons water

cream or vanilla ice cream, to serve

1 Make the pancakes and keep them warm while making the filling. Meanwhile, peel, core and thinly slice the apples.

2 Melt the butter in a frying pan and fry the almonds for 1–2 minutes until golden. Lift them out with a slotted spoon. Add the apples to the pan and fry for 5 minutes until softened.

3 Add the sugar and cook for 1 minute until dissolved. Stir in the lemon juice, sultanas, mixed spice and water. Cook for 1 minute until bubbling.

4 Using the slotted spoon, place a little of the filling down the centre of each pancake and roll it up. Transfer the pancakes to warmed serving plates and drizzle with the syrup remaining in the pan. Scatter with the almonds and serve with cream or ice cream.

Serves 4
Preparation time: **15 minutes, plus making the pancakes**
Cooking time: **15 minutes**

buckwheat pancakes with figs, goats' cheese and honey

8 Buckwheat Pancakes
(*see page* 14)

4 ripe figs

2 tablespoons orange juice

2 tablespoons caster sugar

125 g (4 oz) soft, rindless goats'
cheese

finely grated rind of 1 orange

6 tablespoons chestnut or orange
blossom honey

This unusual combination of ingredients adds up to a very special finale for a summer meal.

1 Make the pancakes and set them aside while making the toppings.

2 Make two deep crossways cuts through each fig, leaving the figs intact at the base, and place them in a lightly greased, shallow ovenproof dish. Open the tops out slightly and sprinkle with the orange juice and 1 tablespoon of the sugar. Bake in a preheated oven, 220°C (425°F), Gas Mark 7, for 15 minutes or until lightly caramelized.

3 While the figs are cooking, wrap the pancakes in foil and put them in the oven for 10 minutes to warm through.

4 Beat the goats' cheese with the orange rind and the remaining sugar until soft. Crumple a pancake on to a warmed serving plate and top with a second crumpled pancake. Repeat with the remaining pancakes on the other serving plates. Top each one with a spoonful of the goats' cheese and a fig.

5 Stir the honey into the juices left in the fig dish and drizzle the mixture over the pancakes.

Serves 4
Preparation time: **10 minutes, plus making the pancakes**
Cooking time: **15 minutes**

crêpes suzette

1 quantity Basic Pancakes
(*see page* 12)

50 g (2 oz) butter

50 g (2 oz) caster sugar

grated rind and juice of 2 oranges

2 tablespoons Grand Marnier

2 tablespoons brandy

crème fraîche, to serve

1 Make the pancakes and set them aside while making the sauce.

2 To make the sauce, melt the butter in a frying pan, add the sugar, orange rind and juice and heat until bubbling. Dip each pancake into the sauce, fold it into quarters and place on a warmed serving dish.

3 Add the Grand Marnier and brandy to the pan; heat gently, then ignite. Pour the flaming liquid over the pancakes and serve immediately with crème fraîche.

Serves 4
Preparation time: **10 minutes, plus making the pancakes**
Cooking time: **10 minutes**

rum and banana pancakes

1 quantity Sweet Pancakes
(*see page* 15)

4 bananas

2 teaspoons lemon juice

2 tablespoons caster sugar, plus extra to serve

2 teaspoons cornflour

150 ml (¼ pint) rum

1 Make the pancakes and keep them warm while making the filling.

2 Mash the bananas with the lemon juice and sugar. Blend the cornflour with the rum in a saucepan. Heat, stirring, until the mixture thickens. Stir in the bananas and cook for 1 minute.

3 Divide the banana mixture between the pancakes. Roll them up, arrange on a warmed serving dish and dust with sugar. Serve at once.

Serves 4
Preparation time: **10 minutes, plus making the pancakes**
Cooking time: **5 minutes**

blackcurrant pancakes

**1 quantity Basic Pancakes
(*see page* 12)**

**300 g (10 oz) fresh blackcurrants or
canned blackcurrants in natural
juice, drained**

2 tablespoons caster sugar

200 ml (7 fl oz) water

50 g (2 oz) unsalted butter

2 tablespoons crème de cassis

2 tablespoons brandy

blackcurrant sprigs, to decorate

1 Make the pancakes and set aside while making the filling.

2 Put the blackcurrants in a heavy-based saucepan and add the sugar and water. Cook over a low heat until the sugar has dissolved, then increase the heat slightly and cook, stirring occasionally, until the blackcurrants have softened. Strain the blackcurrants through a fine sieve, pressing them lightly with the back of a spoon to extract all the juice. Discard the contents of the sieve.

3 Melt the butter in a large heavy-based frying pan. One by one, coat the pancakes with the butter, fold them in half then in half again as they are coated and push them to the side of the pan. Pour the blackcurrant juice into the frying pan and gently spoon it over the pancakes until they are covered.

4 Mix together the crème de cassis and brandy and warm gently. Pour over the pancakes and ignite with a lighted taper. Once the flames have died down, transfer the contents of the pan to warmed dessert plates. Decorate with blackcurrant sprigs and serve immediately.

Serves 4
Preparation time: **10 minutes, plus
    making the pancakes**
Cooking time: **30 minutes**

strawberry pancakes

1 quantity Sweet Pancakes
(*see page* 15)

250 g (8 oz) strawberries, sliced

50 g (2 oz) icing sugar, sifted

4 tablespoons brandy

25 g (1 oz) butter, plus extra
for greasing

Oranges have a natural affinity with strawberries, so an an orange ice cream or sorbet would go very well with these pancakes.

1 Make the pancakes and set them aside while making the filling.

2 To make the filling, mix the strawberries, sugar and 2 tablespoons of the brandy. Cover and chill until it is needed.

3 Divide the strawberry mixture among the pancakes. Fold them into quarters and arrange in a lightly greased, shallow ovenproof dish. Dot with the butter and bake in a preheated oven, 200°C (400°F), Gas Mark 6, for 10 minutes. Warm the remaining brandy, pour it over the pancakes, set it alight and serve.

Serves 4
Preparation time: **10 minutes, plus making the pancakes**
Cooking time: **10 minutes**

cheesecake pancakes
with sour cherry compôte

8 Sweet Pancakes (*see page* 15)

300 g (10 oz) cream cheese

2 teaspoons vanilla essence

25 g (1 oz) caster sugar

finely grated rind of 1 orange

1 egg, lightly beaten

1 egg yolk

oil, for greasing

icing sugar, for dusting

compôte:

75 g (3 oz) caster sugar

150 ml (¼ pint) water

1 cinnamon stick, halved

500 g (1 lb) fresh sour cherries, stoned

1 teaspoon cornflour

1 Make the pancakes and allow them to cool while making the filling.

2 Beat together the cream cheese, vanilla essence and sugar until softened. Add the orange rind, egg and egg yolk and beat until smooth. Place a spoonful in the centre of each pancake. Fold over two sides to enclose the filling, then fold over the other two sides to make parcels.

3 Arrange the pancakes in a lightly greased, shallow ovenproof dish and bake in a preheated oven, 180°C (350°F), Gas Mark 4, for 10 minutes.

4 Meanwhile, make the cherry compôte. Put the sugar into a saucepan with the measured water and heat until the sugar dissolves. Add the cinnamon and cherries and cook gently for 10 minutes or until the cherries have softened but still hold their shape. Blend the cornflour with a little water and add to the pan. Heat gently, stirring, until the compôte has thickened slightly.

5 Transfer the pancakes to serving plates and dust with icing sugar. Serve with the compôte spooned around.

Serves 4
Preparation time: **20 minutes, plus making the pancakes**
Cooking time: **15 minutes**

pineapple and walnut pancakes

8 Sweet Pancakes (*see page* 15)

1 small ripe pineapple

3 oranges

25 g (1 oz) walnuts, chopped

½ teaspoon cornflour

150 ml (¼ pint) freshly squeezed orange juice

3 tablespoons kirsch

oil, for greasing

caster sugar, for dusting

lightly whipped cream, to serve

1 Make the pancakes and set aside while making the filling.

2 Cut the skin from the pineapple. Discard the core and cut the flesh into small pieces. Peel the oranges. Working over a bowl to catch the juices, cut out the segments from between the membranes. Mix the orange segments with the pineapple and walnuts.

3 Blend the cornflour with a little of the orange juice in a small saucepan. Add the remaining juice and any orange juice left in the bowl. Cook gently, stirring until thickened. Stir in the kirsch then stir 4 tablespoons of the sauce into the fruit mixture.

4 Fold a pancake in half, then in half again. Open it out to form a cone and fill with a little of the fruit mixture. Place in a lightly greased, shallow ovenproof dish and repeat with the remaining pancakes. Dust with a little caster sugar and bake in a preheated oven, 200°C (400°F), Gas Mark 6, for 10–15 minutes until heated through.

5 Transfer the pancakes to warmed serving plates. Spoon over the remaining sauce and serve with lightly whipped cream.

Serves 4
Preparation time: **20 minutes, plus making the pancakes**
Cooking time: **15–20 minutes**

apricot and hazelnut pancakes

8 Sweet Pancakes (*see page* 15)

500 g (1 lb) fresh apricots

2 tablespoons lemon juice

50 g (2 oz) light muscovado sugar,
plus extra for sprinkling

1 teaspoon ground cinnamon

50 g (2 oz) hazelnuts, chopped

oil, for greasing

crème fraîche or Greek yogurt,
to serve

1 Make the pancakes and set them aside while making the filling.

2 Halve, stone and thinly slice the apricots. Toss in a bowl with the lemon juice. Spread the sliced apricots over the pancakes and sprinkle with the sugar, cinnamon and hazelnuts. Roll up the pancakes and arrange in a lightly greased, shallow ovenproof dish.

3 Sprinkle the pancakes with a little more sugar and bake in a preheated oven, 190°C (375°F), Gas Mark 5, for 15 minutes. Serve the pancakes warm with crème fraîche or yogurt.

Serves 4
Preparation time: **15 minutes, plus making the pancakes**
Cooking time: **15 minutes**

melba pancakes

8 Sweet Pancakes (*see page* 15)

2 tablespoons lemon juice

4 tablespoons icing sugar

4 ripe peaches, skinned, stoned and sliced

150 g (5 oz) raspberries

crème fraîche and honey, to serve

1 Make the pancakes. Drizzle 4 of them with the lemon juice and sprinkle with 3 tablespoons of the icing sugar. Cover each pancake with a second one and then scrunch them up into rounds about 15 cm (6 inch) in diameter. Transfer to a lightly greased baking sheet and bake in a preheated oven, 200°C (400°F), Gas Mark 6, for 6–8 minutes until hot.

2 Transfer the pancakes to warmed serving plates. Scatter with the peach slices and raspberries and top with crème fraîche and a drizzle of honey. Dust with the remaining sugar and serve immediately.

Serves 4
Preparation time: **10 minutes, plus making the pancakes**
Cooking time: **6–8 minutes**

lemon soufflé pancakes

8 Basic Pancakes (*see page* 12)

25 g (1 oz) butter, plus extra for greasing

25 g (1 oz) plain flour

300 ml (½ pint) milk

25 g (1 oz) caster sugar

grated rind and juice of 1 lemon

2 eggs, separated, plus 1 extra egg white

25 g (1 oz) icing sugar

1 Make the pancakes and set aside while making the filling.

2 To make the filling, melt the butter in a saucepan, stir in the flour and cook gently for 2–3 minutes. Add the milk, sugar and lemon rind and juice. Bring to the boil, stirring until thickened. Cool slightly then beat in the egg yolks. Whisk the egg whites until stiff and fold them into the mixture.

3 Fill and fold the pancakes and arrange them in a lightly greased, shallow ovenproof dish. Dust with icing sugar. Bake in a preheated oven, 200°C (400°F), Gas Mark 6, for 10–15 minutes.

Serves 4
Preparation time: **20 minutes, plus making the pancakes**
Cooking time: **20–25 minutes**

praline almond pancakes

50 g (2 oz) ground almonds, toasted

1 teaspoon almond essence

5 tablespoons milk

1 quantity Basic Pancake batter (*see page* 12)

oil or butter, for frying

75 g (3 oz) caster sugar, plus extra for sprinkling

5 tablespoons water

75 g (3 oz) whole blanched almonds

175 g (6 oz) unsalted butter, softened

cream or ice cream, to serve

1 Beat the ground almonds, almond essence and milk into the basic batter and cook the pancakes following the instructions on page 12.

2 Brush a small baking sheet with oil. To make the filling, put the sugar in a small heavy-based saucepan with the water. Heat gently, stirring until the sugar has completely dissolved, then bring the syrup to the boil and cook, tilting the pan occasionally, until it has turned to a golden caramel. Immediately remove the pan from the heat, stir in the blanched almonds and pour on to the baking sheet. Leave until it is brittle.

3 Place the nut mixture in a polythene bag and beat with a rolling pin to break it into small pieces. Transfer to a food processor or blender and grind until finely chopped.

4 Beat the butter in a bowl until softened, then stir in the nut mixture. Spread the almond paste over the pancakes and roll them up. Arrange in a lightly greased, shallow ovenproof dish and sprinkle with a little extra sugar. Bake in a preheated oven, 190°C (375°F), Gas Mark 5, for 10 minutes until warmed through. Serve warm with cream or ice cream.

Serves 6
Preparation time: **20 minutes, plus making the pancake batter**
Cooking time: **35 minutes**

pancakes with hazelnut sauce

1 quantity Basic Pancake batter
(*see page* 12)

oil or butter, for frying

filling:

175 g (6 oz) ground hazelnuts

300 ml (½ pint) double cream

75 g (3 oz) icing sugar

These sweet and satisfying pancakes have a rich and nutty flavour, perfect for autumn and winter parties.

1 Make the batter. Lightly grease a 25 cm (10 inch) frying pan and cook 4 large pancakes following the instructions on page 12. Keep them warm while you make the filling.

2 To make the filling, mix together half of the hazelnuts, 4 tablespoons of the cream and half of the icing sugar. Divide the filling among the pancakes and roll up. Place on a warmed serving dish.

3 Gently heat the remaining hazelnuts, cream and icing sugar in a saucepan and pour over the pancakes.

Makes 4
Preparation time: **15 minutes, plus making the batter**
Cooking time: **15 minutes**

pancakes with chestnut cream and amaretto

1 quantity Basic Pancakes (*see page* 12)

chestnut cream:

250 g (8 oz) unsweetened chestnut purée

grated rind of 1 orange, plus extra to decorate

2 tablespoons Amaretto di Saronno

2 tablespoons sugar

300 ml (½ pint) cream

chestnut syrup:

300 ml (½ pint) maple syrup

175 g (6 oz) cooked chestnuts, finely chopped

2 tablespoons Amaretto di Saronno

Any liqueur may be used in this recipe; try experimenting with Cointreau, Drambuie or brandy.

1 Make the pancakes and keep them warm while making the filling.

2 To make the chestnut cream, put the chestnut purée into a large bowl with the orange rind, Amaretto and sugar and mix together. In another bowl, whip the cream until it forms soft peaks. Fold the cream into the chestnut mixture and refrigerate until needed.

3 To make the chestnut syrup, heat the maple syrup and chopped chestnuts in a saucepan, bring to the boil and stir in the Amaretto. Remove the warm pancakes from the oven, and the chestnut cream from the refrigerator. Fill each pancake with some chestnut cream, roll it up, and arrange on a individual plate or a warmed serving platter. Drizzle the heated syrup over the pancakes and serve immediately decorated with grated orange rind.

Serves 4
Preparation time: **15 minutes, plus making the pancakes**
Cooking time: **10 minutes**

chocolate and banana pancake torte

50 g (2 oz) ground hazelnuts or almonds, toasted

1 teaspoon almond essence

4 tablespoons milk

1 quantity Sweet Pancake batter (*see page* 15)

oil or butter, for frying

300 g (10 oz) chocolate and hazelnut spread

4 tablespoons double cream

5 large bananas

2 tablespoons lemon juice

icing sugar, for sprinkling

25 g (1 oz) hazelnuts, toasted and roughly chopped

single cream, to serve

Although delicious served at room temperature, this dessert can also be warmed through before serving. Assemble it on a baking sheet instead of a plate and warm through in a preheated oven, 200°C (400°F), Gas Mark 6, for 10 minutes.

1 Beat the ground nuts, almond essence and milk into the pancake batter and cook the pancakes following the instructions on page 15. Set the pancakes aside while making the filling.

2 Put the chocolate spread in a small pan with the cream and heat gently until slightly softened but not liquid. Slice the bananas as thinly as possible and toss in the lemon juice.

3 Place a pancake on a flat plate and spread with a little of the chocolate spread. Cover with a thin layer of banana slices. Arrange another pancake on top. Continue layering the ingredients, finishing with a pancake. Sprinkle with icing sugar and scatter with toasted hazelnuts. Serve cut into wedges with cream.

Serves 6
Preparation time: **20 minutes, plus making the pancake batter**
Cooking time: **25 minutes**

baked pancakes
with glossy chocolate sauce

1 quantity Basic Pancakes
(*see page* 12)

250 g (8 oz) ricotta cheese

3 tablespoons caster sugar

150 g (5 oz) fresh or frozen
blueberries, thawed

3 packets of white chocolate
buttons

4 tablespoons double cream

glossy chocolate sauce:

125 g (4 oz) caster sugar

100 ml (3½ fl oz) water

200 g (7 oz) plain chocolate,
broken into pieces

25 g (1 oz) unsalted butter, plus
extra for greasing

Use a chocolate with a high cocoa butter content to make a rich and delicious sauce.

1 Make the pancakes and set them aside while making the filling.

2 To make the filling, mix together the ricotta, sugar, blueberries, white chocolate buttons and cream.

3 Thinly spread the filling over the pancakes then fold them into quarters and arrange in a greased, shallow ovenproof dish. Cook in a preheated oven, 190°C (375°F), Gas Mark 5, for 8–10 minutes until warmed through.

4 Meanwhile, make the sauce. Heat the caster sugar and water in a small heavy-based saucepan until the sugar has dissolved. Bring the syrup to the boil and boil rapidly for 1 minute. Remove the pan from the heat and add the chocolate. Leave until melted, then stir in the butter to make a smooth glossy sauce. Serve hot, with the filled pancakes.

Serves 4
Preparation time: **20 minutes, plus making the pancakes**
Cooking time: **8–10 minutes**

hot chocolate pancakes
with spiced ricotta and raisins

1 quantity Chocolate Pancakes (*see page* 17)

1 quantity Glossy Chocolate Sauce (*see page* 62)

lightly whipped cream, to serve (optional)

filling:

1 piece of stem ginger, about 15 g (½ oz), finely chopped

2 tablespoons caster sugar, plus extra for dusting

250 g (8 oz) ricotta cheese

50 g (2 oz) raisins

150 g (5 oz) white chocolate, finely chopped

3 tablespoons double cream

1 Make the pancakes and set them aside while making the filling.

2 To make the filling, mix the ginger in a bowl with the sugar, ricotta, raisins, white chocolate and cream. Place spoonfuls of the filling in the centres of the pancakes and fold them into quarters, enclosing the filling.

3 Place the pancakes in a lightly greased, shallow ovenproof dish and dust with sugar. Bake in a preheated oven, 200°C (400°F), Gas Mark 6, for 10 minutes until heated through. Serve hot with the glossy chocolate sauce and cream, if liked.

Serves 4
Preparation time: **20 minutes, plus making the pancakes and the chocolate sauce**
Cooking time: **about 10 minutes**

index